THE SIX SENSES

THE SIX SENSES

Cassandra Atherton
Paul Hetherington
Paul Munden
Jen Webb
Jordan Williams

authorised theft

The Six Senses
authorised theft / Recent Work Press
Canberra, Australia

This chapbook series was produced with the support of the
International Poetry Studies Institute (IPSI), based within the
Centre for Creative and Cultural Research, Faculty of Arts and
Design, University of Canberra.
http://ipsi.org.au

Collection © Recent Work Press 2019
The copyright of the individual poems remains with the authors.
Design: Caren Florance

ISBN 978-0-6485537-9-3

recentworkpress.com

Introduction	Paul Hetherington	vii
Research Statement	Jen Webb	ix
TOUCH	Cassandra Atherton	1
SMELL	Paul Hetherington	27
SOUND	Paul Munden	51
THE SIXTH SENSE	Jen Webb	75
TASTE	Jordan Williams	99
CITE		111
ABOUT THE POETS		121

The AUTHORISED THEFT series of poetry chapbooks was initiated by the International Poetry Studies Institute (IPSI) based in the Faculty of Arts and Design at the University of Canberra. The first collection of chapbooks – Cassandra Atherton's Pegs, *Paul Hetherington's* Jars, *Paul Munden's* Keys, *Jen Webb's* Gaps *and Jordan Williams'* Nets *– resulted from discussions connected to IPSI's Prose Poetry Project, inaugurated by IPSI in late 2014. A second collection,* The Taoist Elements, *followed in 2016; a third,* Colours, *in 2017; and a fourth,* Prosody, *in 2018. This fifth collection builds on the same creative collaboration. IPSI supports and promotes collaborative and collegiate poetic work in a variety of forms, and encourages the collaboration of poets with other artists, such as Caren Florance who has designed the series.*

THE SIX SENSES: AN INTRODUCTION
Paul Hetherington

This fifth collection of AUTHORISED THEFT chapbooks builds on the spirit of creative collaboration that has always been so much part of the IPSI ethos and – in a change to the previous format – collates all five chapbooks in a single volume. The five chapbooks explore ideas and emotions associated with the six senses – sight, sound, smell, touch, taste, and the mysterious and elusive 'sixth sense'. Sensory perception and knowledge are crucial to human activity but are often taken for granted and modern life bombards us with sensory stimulae to such an extent that we may sometimes feel the need to escape from the smelly hubbub and visual cacophony of our lives. In such circumstances we are often trying to neutralise or negate what our sense impressions tell us. Yet the senses are so profoundly important that we could barely exist without them. When we pay attention to them, we often find ourselves attuned to what is subtle, aesthetically pleasing and especially suggestive – or pungent and unpleasant.

Even in the womb, and always thereafter, our senses help us navigate the world. We learn to know ourselves and our environments through the senses, fashioning identity and memory from sensory experience as much as through what other people actively teach us. Further, from an early age, sense perceptions inform crucial aspects of our important relationships. We know other people not only through what they say of themselves but through complex sense impressions related to their appearance, the particular qualities of their voice and even how they smell. The senses also play a significant role in intimate relationships, not least because the quality of a person's touch informs many aspects of lovemaking.

Memory encodes some sense impressions so powerfully that we are capable of recollecting whole scenes and occasions simply through encountering a sensory association. Marcel Proust famously conjured memory out of the taste of a madeleine dipped in tea, writing:

> when from a long-distant past nothing subsists, after the people are dead, after the things are broken and scattered, taste and smell alone, more fragile but more enduring, more immaterial, more persistent, more faithful, remain poised a long time, like souls, remembering, waiting, hoping, amid the ruins of all the rest; and bear unflinchingly, in the tiny and almost impalpable drop of their essence, the vast structure of recollection. (2005: 54)

Similar statements may be made for all of the senses. Sometimes, the tonality of a piece of music will haunt a person for a lifetime; occasionally an experience of touch will be a profound kind of transport; certain images have the capacity to become deeply symbolic and even iconic; and our 'sixth sense' tells us that there are always important things beyond our ken.

All five authors of these chapbooks have delved into their chosen 'sense' to find new and creative ways of remembering, knowing, imagining and understanding taste, touch, smell, sound and the sixth sense – and all have also alluded to the sense of sight. Sight may not be the specific, named subject of a chapbook in this series but, in one way or another, it is addressed by all of them. Each of these chapbooks 'sees' in a variety of ways; and, as it does so, each also emphasises the extraordinariness of hearing, touching, smelling, tasting and intuiting the world. Each emphasises how prose poetry may reach towards the ineffable, conjure desire, present the desiring subject and reinflect sensory experiences in language that reaches beyond grammar and denotation into the elusive world that the six senses powerfully understand.

Works cited

Proust, M 2005 *In search of lost time*. Vol I: *Swann's Way* (trans CK Scott Moncrieff and T Kilmartin, rev DJ Enright), London: Vintage

THE SIX SENSES: RESEARCH STATEMENT

Jen Webb

The senses have long been used by poets and mystics as allegorical tools, or metaphorical vehicles: as means to traverse the space between the abstract domain of language, and what is beyond that domain: the material world, or 'the real'. For many philosophers and semiologists, there is an irreducible gap between language and the real, because language does not call into presence the object being named, but only gestures toward it – by inference (Eco 1984), by relations of difference between signifiers (Derrida 1976), or by questions of equivalence (Voloshinov 1930). Language, that is, *makes* meaning, but it does not and cannot reliably represent the material world. This is not to say that world is outside human experience: as Catherine Belsey (2007: n.p.) observes, 'all knowledges are subject to limits, and the real is what resides outside those limits, but may have consequences in people's lives, just the same'. We are formed and framed by the physical and experiential as much as we are by language and culture, and we know in ways that cannot be fully explicated in words.

For Maurice Merleau-Ponty (1968), it is the body rather than consciousness that is site and source of knowledge; and this is where the senses become most effective: first the five senses identified by Aristotle (1907) – sight, touch, taste, hearing and smell – and the 'other one', known as the 'sixth sense', and applied to a range of sensory and extra-sensory perceptions that seem to exceed the tangible and material experience offered by the other five. Now there are at least ten senses named by physiological scientists, and all are modes in which the body orients itself to, recognises, and engages with the external world. Aristotle would be pleased by this: it is now de rigueur to trace the ways in which what he terms 'the sensible object' (the stimulus) (425b24–426a19, p.115) and the human connect to make experience live. But Aristotle takes the human responsibility further than medical science: for most of the senses, according to science, the body's knowing and orientation takes place without our conscious awareness. But for Aristotle, showing early signs of phenomenological curiosity, the sensory matters because it makes sense when the human is what he calls a 'percipient subject' (425b24–426a19, p.115) – an aware human, paying attention to the stimulus. Language 'fails in its task' (Prendergast 2000: 2), but the living body makes meanings and understandings. Poetry comes into its own here, focused as it is on the sensory, on expressing the inexpressible, and on the ineffable. For Alice Oswald (2000: 37), 'the whole challenge of poetry is to keep language open, so that what we don't yet know can pass through it'. This collection of chapbooks aims to keep language open, and to pay close attention to the sensory, to its stimuli, and to our responses to the unrepresentable world in which we have our being.

Works cited

Aristotle 1907 [c350BCE] *De Anima* Book II (trans RD Hicks), Cambridge: Cambridge University Press

Belsey, C in interview with Karen Hall and David Nel 2007 'Attention to language', *Limina: A Journal of Historical and Cultural Studies* 13: 1–9

Derrida, J 1976 *Of Grammatology* (trans G Spivak), Baltimore, MD: John Hopkins University Press

Eco, U 1984 *Semiotics and the Philosophy of Language*, London: Macmillan

Merleau-Ponty, Maurice 1968 *The Visible and the Invisible* (trans A Lingis), Evanston, IL: Northwestern University Press

Oswald, A 2000 'The universe in time of rain makes the world alive with noise', in Sarah Maguire (ed), *A Green Thought in a Green Shade: Poetry in the Garden*, London: The Poetry Society, 35–48

Prendergast, C 2000 *The Triangle of Representation*, New York, NY: Columbia University Press

Voloshinov, VN 1973 [1930] *Marxism and the Philosophy of Language* (trans L Matejka and IR Titunik), New York & London: Seminar Press

TOUCH

Cassandra Atherton

'At the touch of love, everyone becomes a poet.'
—*Plato*

'Touch has a memory. O say, love, say,
What can I do to kill it and be free?'
—*John Keats*

5	Dentist
6	Violinist
7	Danseur
8	Pilot
9	Ex-Priest
10	Art Collector
11	Calligrapher
12	Shakespearean Actor
13	Best Friend's Father
14	Professional Netflix Watcher
15	Freelance Fortune Cookie Writer
16	Therapist
17	Tinker
18	Tailor
19	Solider
20	Sailor
21	Rich Man
22	Poor Man
23	Beggar Man
24	Thief
25	Curator

DENTIST

It started when I caught you fingering my x-rays, tracing the outline of each tooth with a wet index finger. You asked me to show you my brush stroke, placed your hand over mine as I moved the bristles across my front teeth. Up and down. I watched in the mirror as you closed your eyes and leant into me. At my six-monthly check-up you asked if you could make a mould of my mouth, placing a tray of putty over my top teeth. You said I had an excellent gag reflex. As you held the little mirror in my mouth, you confided in me your fear of hotel toothbrushes: their coarseness, their small heads and the way they abraded the enamel. You unclipped my bib and took off my sunglasses. I said, 'I've always preferred soft bristles,' and you kissed me, your rubber gloved hands on my face. When we made love, you liked to slip your finger between my teeth as I bit down. Later, you examined the straight blunt lines of my front teeth and deep, enduring spots of my incisors, running your tongue over the grooves and ridges. You left when I chipped my front tooth playing netball. I switched my dental floss for two bags of fairy floss and went to bed without brushing.

VIOLINIST

I liked it when you said 'Stradivarius' in the dark. And the odd way you said 'Pachelbel's Canon' with a long sounding pash at the beginning. For three years on Saturdays I'd come to your apartment and eat iced vovos while you played Shostakovich's Trio No. 2. Until the cut on your finger opened and dropped blood on your fingerboard. Sometimes you'd reward me by playing *The Devil Went Down to Georgia* and I'd dance around the living room singing, 'Fire on the Mountain, run boys, run!' You'd put your violin in its case and lick rogue flakes of coconut from my eyelashes. In bed I called you Paganini, whispering 'devil's violinist' in your ear as you played my backbone. Twelve bones per second. I loved the feel of the calluses where your violin rested below the angle of your jaw and above your collarbone. I nuzzled their redness while your finger pizzicatoed up the back of my thigh. I liked it when you ran your bow across the sheen of my hair, imagining the music. But as you played the single string in the cadenza, I realised you didn't need any accompaniment.

DANSEUR

My toes felt like they were suffocating, but I loved the feeling of their confinement. A tiny box of wood packaging my toes. A parcel of toes. A gift of toes. I internalised the sound the toe box made on a wooden floor; a muffled knocking. You told me it meant I was on *the primrose way to the everlasting bonfire* and asked me to rest my feet in your lap. I asked what you were wearing under your tights. At rehearsal, you traced the long, fine marks the floorboards left on my thighs, your index finger edging under the hem of my ballet skirt. We fouetted side by side, until the walls were lime and I thought of nut whirls and *Quality Street* chocolates in brightly coloured wrappers. In the pas de deux your breath was hot on the tip of my ear; your neck nook smelt like rosin. There was an unmade king-size bed in your bedroom, a white duvet piled in the centre like a Mr Whippy ice-cream. You asked me to dance while you took opera glasses from the top drawer in your bedside bureau and trained them on my feet. Scopophilia. Afterwards, you lined up your index finger with my spine, a frisson of bone on bone and I became your soft serve. You said, 'Parts of each of us stand in for a whole.' But we were never joined at the hip. You stroked my thirty-three vertebrae until my spinal cord started to vibrate. You ruptured the moment by stroking my high instep until my toe joints ached with pleasure. A year later, when you made a clean break, my cross-training prevented stress fractures.

PILOT

There was something about a cockpit, something about its root meaning. *A pit of fighting cocks.* Poe-esque. Like the pit and the pendulum, but with cocks. Deplaning from a flight to Boston, you asked me if I'd like to see the flight deck; touch your flight instruments. You steered me into the cockpit like I was attached to your tiller, telling me to follow my nose wheel. The golden stripes on your sleeves and the celestial wings on your hat were backed in deep blue. You slid into the pilot's seat, tiny computer screens moving with maps and measurements. I liked the switches on the roof; you wanted to show me your thrust lever. But every time we had sex it was like you were on autopilot. I wanted some throttle but you always seemed to need guidance. You said our relationship had too much of a negative feedback loop. I told you the experience was a real yaw dampener. I'll miss the Krug in the first-class lounge for breakfast and the iconic deconstructed pavlova in a glass, served with seasonal fruits and topped with Persian fairy floss but I need more hands-on approach whereas you liked to watch.

EX-PRIEST

You used to touch me like a chalice taken from a tabernacle after Sunday Mass; shiny and precious vessel. I was your transubstantiation project. More of a fish than a loaf. More of a mustard seed than a fig tree. I liked it when you said the word 'sacristy' because it sounded like 'sacred' and 'Christ' all mixed up. I made you whisper 'sacristy' in my ear. It somehow sounded profane. You gave me a first edition of *The Thorn Birds* for my birthday and called me Meggie for two years. I watched the miniseries and bought a dress called Ashes of Roses. You laughed when I justified *Fame* as a Liturgical dance; 'I want to live forever', a comment on Christ's immortality. I asked why you left the Jesuits when they are the smartest of all priests and Saint Ignatius of Loyola was sexy. You told me you could still be smart and hot without being a Jesuit. But, as it turned out, I liked men who keep their vows; no amount of impaling myself on your thorn could change that.

ART COLLECTOR

You called my bruises paintings; saw their yellow and purple hue as paint on the canvas of my Impressionist thighs. If I can't be Lizzie Siddal or Jeanne Hébuterne, I choose Victorine Meurent. She was all shoes and flowers as Olympia; all creamy skin and white bed sheets. The first time we had sex, you laid me sideways across the bed. The flower in my hair came to rest on the floor between your sock and my underwear. But you filtered life through art; responded to the artist who squeezed your heart the tightest. Five weeks and four days later, I didn't stand a chance.

CALLIGRAPHER

I like to be written on; savour the feeling of long lines of sticky ink trailing across my skin. Turning me blue-black; black and blue. I wrote about it once; about the way I liked my lovers to inscribe their names on me. So that even when ink washed away, the signatures would be detectable under black light; ultra-violet. You loved my indelible secrets; wrote them in Kanji on my stomach with a bamboo brush. Flourishes of deep ink softly branded me; pine soot ink fluttering on my solar plexus. You were careful about the angle of the brush; started and closed off each character with a perfect parallelogram. You painted the horizontal strokes first and proceeded left to right, top to bottom, drawing tiny arrows to show me the direction of each line. For a time, my flesh was your washi; your pillow book. As you wrote, I rotated; your human scroll. When I was covered in your markings, we made love and you read my narratives into the night; a literate *oshouji*. Later, as I slept, you left to find an unmarked canvas.

SHAKESPEAREAN ACTOR

I love Laurence Olivier. Larry. Larry O. Ohhh. When I was younger I wanted to be Scarlett O'Hara. Not Vivien Leigh. I wanted to be a nymphet. Not a nymphomaniac. With a dress made out of curtains. Velvet and lush. Like Scarlett's moss green curtain dress. A dress made out of lies. Like the Caroline de Winter dress in *Rebecca*. Larry wanted Viv to play Mrs De Winter II. But she was too beautiful – she was a Rebecca not an unnamed narrator. I first saw you at an ephemera fair in Camberwell. You were bidding on a signed photograph of Larry and Viv on their visit to Australia. Later, I was cast as Ophelia to your Hamlet in the Melbourne University Shakespeare Company. I was more Vivien Leigh than Jean Simmons but your performance captured Olivier's fierce egotism. You liked us to recite our lines when we had sex. *You jig and amble, and you lisp, you nickname God's creatures and make your wantonness your ignorance.* You tugged on my plaits as I writhed beneath you. *Hey non nonny, nonny, hey nonny.* You said iambic pentameter was the language of desire; the da-DUM of the human heartbeat. But your fingers in my hair were glass and I was the only *watchman to my heart.* da-DUM. We split when you told me you believed Christopher Marlowe had faked his own death and written Shakespeare's plays and poems. da-DUM. I took the signed photo of Larry and Viv and in its place left the note, *O what a noble mind is here o'erthrown*, and a sprig of rosemary.

BEST FRIEND'S FATHER

You were tossing pizza dough. White spheres like Salvadore Dali's plates spinning above your head. Edible frisbees. I was reminded of those circus performers who spin tableware on sticks. Like small space ships. You had six on the go, tossing them high – 'I hope you're staying for dinner' – flinging me a circle of floury dough. It stretched over my hands like dough gloves. I helped you press it into a shiny pizza pan and you swirled tomato paste. I dressed mine with olives, artichokes and jalapeños; you called them shiny wet things. We'd twice had sex in your car; red vinyl seats clinging to my shins, the air freshener swinging back and forth on your rear vision mirror. I liked how you called me *fragolina* and interlaced your fingers across the small of my back. Your daughter balanced each pizza on a large wooden paddle and you helped her slide it into the woodfire oven. There was too much pizza in that cave of heat, but you thought it was always better to have too much than not enough. Or even enough. Enough didn't prepare for the future. Enough was as careless as not enough. For seven months, I watched you sneak my leftover crusts from my plate; put your mouth where mine had been; eat my teeth marks. Then you'd drive me home and I'd play your Daliesque *coeur de fraises* and bare my back for your lattice finger work. For me enough was enough.

PROFESSIONAL NETFLIX WATCHER

Sometimes I'd curl so far into you, I'd leave behind a huge expanse of bed. When I fell asleep, you'd get up and slip into that space, watching a Netflix film on your iphone. Sometimes I pushed my pillow up close and snuggled into your back – you had little dimples on either side of your lower spine. I knew the best places for my head to rest: the hollow above your collarbone; the crannies of your chest. When we watched films on your laptop, I rested my chin on the soft part of your thigh. But you said it was pointy. You called it 'chinning'. Once we binge watched all of the first season of *You* with my chin just above your knee. Neither of us moved for so long, the message 'Are you still watching?' popped up on the screen. You moved and there was a blue sideways oval on your leg. I rubbed my chin in sympathy but you were shaking your leg and saying you had no feeling below your knee. You called me a 'chinner'; said my chin had cut off your circulation and you'd have to get the bottom half of your leg amputated. I said you should choose something comic. So, we watched eleven seasons of *Cheers* in a blanket burrito and drank beer until morning. Rather than skipping the credits on the final episode, you let them roll while you pulled me under you, singing the theme song in falsetto as I wriggled out of my pyjama pants. On Netflix the credits only go for fifteen seconds but you still finished before they ended.

FREELANCE FORTUNE COOKIE WRITER

Shaped like a sickle moon or the crease in a fedora, my fortune cookie was my big easy. Crescent city. Moon, prism, power. After finishing my eggplant tofu, I cracked it open: *The fortune you seek is in another cookie.* Olly olly oxen free. Hide and seek. It wasn't inaccurate. My ex-boyfriend said I was rarely satisfied. I ate the cookie and screwed up the fortune. You were sitting at the table behind me. Double orange chicken with fried rice and chow mien. 'No-one eats the fortune cookie,' you said. But I said they tasted like ice-cream cones – wafer not waffle. Only 20 calories. I saw your unopened cookie. 'Can I have your fortune?' You broke open the cookie and handed me the paper: *Two can live as cheaply as one, for half as long.* 'I think your fortune cookie is propositioning me,' I said. 'Smart cookie,' you replied. You didn't tell me you wrote cookie fortunes for a living until our third date. You boasted about two of your most popular axioms: *The early bird gets the worm, but the second mouse gets the cheese. No snowflake in an avalanche ever feels responsible.* I went home with you then because I liked cheese and snow. Blue and white. Hard and soft. Sometimes soft and hard. But you made love like you wrote fortunes. Succinctly. Generically. I went back to *Panda Express* and ordered vegetable spring rolls. My fortune cookie said: *You will be hungry again in one hour.*

THERAPIST

You charged me two-hundred and ninety dollars an hour. Every Friday at four. Four 'til five. Except I was usually late. You didn't pounce right away; made me go through fifty hypothetical scenarios and relational psychology tests. You said, 'your home is representative of your ambition' and 'the Olympic swimming pool you imagined in your backyard is related to the size of your sexual drive'. You waited until I'd read Marie Cardinal's *The Words To Say It* and DM Thomas's *The White Hotel* and had taken the online quiz – 'Over achiever'. After the island scenario – I'd chosen *Robinson Crusoe* for the irony – you joined me on the couch, one hand rhythmically mussing up my hair as you kissed my naked earlobes and unzipped your pants. Twelve minutes later I left your office with a cup of water from your cooler and a box of tissues. Five o'clock. The following Friday I asked if you had a diagnosis for me. As you buckled your belt and left me on the couch, you told me I had a fear of abandonment. You gave me a 25% discount, closed my file and wrote across the front: *Rx penis normalis, repetatur.*

TINKER

You called me your Tinkerbell; used a dam to patch my tin heart. I was a bricolage of men's alloyed promises and you rasped and smoothed them down; gave me a satin finish. In your hands, my back was a timpani of bones; my ribs a hollow stock pot. As you tinkered with my scapula, I told you if I was a pan, I'd be a cocotte – so you pulled me on top of you until I boiled over. I asked you to stay, told you my favourite character as a child was always Saucepan Man, but you said you needed to move on – solder someone else's tin heart. I lied and told you I didn't give a tinker's cuss.

TAILOR

Your hands spanned my ribcage, fingertips digging into the shallow spaces between my bones – leaving red spots on my skin. You were rash. I came down with lover's measles. Your tape measure was a cold strip from collarbone to waist. You measured the circumference of my left ankle; the space between freckles. I measured the breaths between heartbeats; the sighs between espresso shots in green and orange cups. You pushed me against the architrave, balanced a ruler above my head and made a biro mark in the shiny paint. Five feet four in stilettos. Louboutin for the red sole. Soul mate. Like my bleeding heart. I took the tape from your pocket and measured your inner seam. You dressed to the left; my nerve centre throbbed on the right. Naked as an Empress, I was unstitched as you sewed.

SOLDIER

On the last day, I made you chewy Anzac cookies and we watched the sunrise to the stark strains of 'The Last Post'. Apricot light was a soundwave feathering outwards from the horizon. I reached up and removed a stray oat from the corner of your mouth.

SAILOR

You said I had mermaid hair so I plaited a long, thin strand and placed it around your neck; a peach-coloured garland. I told you I was like Glynis Johns in *Miranda*; you said I was more tempestuous. An Ariel to your Ahab. A Lorelei to your Sinbad. At night you recited 'The Rime of the Ancient Mariner' while I ate spaghetti marinara and flew around your bedroom like an albatross. But when you turned off the lights I became your siren; a pulsing threnody. Under a canopy of my hair, you stroked my breasts and kissed the dip between my neck and collarbone until I foundered. Before you pulled anchor and sailed away, you said I'd always be your silver girl.

RICH MAN

In the late 90s I was your sugar baby; your jam tart. You flew me to Sydney for dinner and to Tahiti on long weekends. On cool nights you covered me with your body. I was your manic pixie dream girl before it was a trope – your Holly Golightly; your Patricia Franchini; your Sugar 'Kane' Kowalczyk. You fed me oysters, caviar and poisson cru and tucked frangipanis behind my right ear – sunset plumeria with pink and yellow stripes. In the morning you watched me stir caster sugar into my cola and eat gummy bears in threes; you said, 'come here and give me some sugar'. I reached across and caressed the bottom left part of your ear lobe – a miniature apricot hanging from a golden tree. I ran the pad of my index finger across your lips and licked your cheek. Prickly pear. Custard apple. When you nuzzled my nape you said I smelt like peach fizz; whispered 'baby peach bubbles' into the dark. But you became hyperglycemic and not even my candy striper outfit was enough to persuade you.

POOR MAN

We bonded over tinned butter beans and home-brand non-fat Greek yoghurt. I had a huge bag of rice in my trolley and you had a sack of unwashed potatoes. I was a kipfler girl, loved the creaminess of their flesh; their waxy finger-shape. You preferred desirees because they reminded you of Tennessee Williams and sultry nights. I liked gratin dauphinoise and fondant potatoes but you preferred hasselback and jacket. I made scalloped and your favourite were mashed. We collided in a cloud of carbohydrates. Hale and hearty. You were all heart; bought Valentine's Day cards in bulk – two decades of *I love you* for $5.95. You purchased rolls of one-ply toilet paper by the dozen; prawn flavoured two-minute noodles by the pallet. But you were generous in bed and liberal with your kisses; spent your time trailing fingertips between my breasts and paying me compliments. One night, after sex, you ended it by saying I wasn't cheap enough to be a really good deal.

BEGGAR MAN

Your *please please*s in the bedroom were polite but insistent. I kissed every spot you implored me to, and slipped my arm across your chest as you slept. When you beseeched me to choose the apple crumble rather than the cherry pie, I acquiesced – even though I hate cinnamon and dislike apples. I watched you drink Glowtinis all night after I gave in to your entreaties to be designated driver. But when you said it would be a mistake to leave you, I begged to differ.

THIEF

When you told me you were a cat burglar, I warned you I was an animal activist. You said you didn't steal cats. But I wanted to know where you stashed your felines and what your intentions were. 'Pure breeds or tabbies?' 'I'm the Cat,' you said, 'like Cary Grant in *To Catch a Thief*.' You took two velvet cases from a hollowed hardcopy of *The Unbearable Lightness of Being*. The first contained a tennis bracelet; white diamonds on a white gold chain. You clasped it around my wrist. The second box contained a Harry Winston necklace. 'One hundred and ninety-five marquise and pear-shaped diamonds, weighing a total of 136.66 carats, set in platinum.' I lifted my hair and you kissed my nape before securing it around my neck. It was cold and heavy on my collarbone. 'What then shall you choose?' you asked unzipping my dress, 'weight or lightness?' My body heat warmed the platinum; I was an electrical conductor, crackling under your fingertips. Your hot breath misted the diamonds on my décolletage. 'Love begins at the point when a woman enters her first word into our poetic memory,' you said expectantly. But I remained silent. The following night I was woken by sirens. I got a cat and gave it a diamond collar.

CURATOR

My body is a palimpsest of ex-lovers. Slowly, you overwrite the markings of every other kiss with your lips, your hands making their way down my body. You begin by smoothing down my flyaway hair and end by stroking my dancer's instep. My skin records the trail, striking through everything that has come before. You cover me in one afternoon's bliss, a superimposition of desire in permanent marker on my flesh. It cannot be undone.

SMELL

Paul Hetherington

'Through the open door, stealthily, came the scent of madonna lilies, almost as if it were prowling abroad.'
—*DH Lawrence*

30	Collection
31	Basil
32	Oil
33	Handwriting
34	Spices
35	Garlic
36	Light
37	Sap
38	Mineral Salts
39	Wood Smoke
40	Bitter Lemon
41	Fumes
42	Lipstick
43	Walls
44	Language
45	Vinyl
46	Cups
47	Fold
45	Furrow
49	Aroma
50	Perfumery

COLLECTION

I began to curate when only sixteen, catching the aroma of newly bought flip flops. Today, ten thousand are locked in containers, hermetically sealed. Pheromones captured from bees mid-flight; purplish bouquets of fading red wine; the grassy complexity of an ancient champagne. Jealousy, too, with its bitter-green savour; washes of water from a ferry's waste pipes. I have sweat from poets about to recite; and fumes of plastic just out of the mould; the splashing aroma of a jumped-upon puddle. Dog hairs have yielded five of my scents; so, too, the blood of a wounded soldier. My favourite is a hint of meringue I found on a shoe in a park in rain. A message of sorts from the wide-speaking world. Sweetness, staleness and wet abandonment.

BASIL

The smell of basil on her fingers is a journey to ancient empires. As is the bend of her back; and the silver glitter in her eyes, provoking thoughts of the Sassanid Empire. Travelling silk roads through Italy, Greece and Turkey, heading south to the Cape of Spices and the Arabian Sea, then to Taxila before skirting the northern reaches of the Plateau of Tibet. That long, shushing utterance in her mouth.

OIL

In an ancient city we're ensconced in baths that smell of time's exposures; of salt and bodies. A woman holds my arm. There are no verities; shadows close out an afternoon. Tomorrow there'll be fireworks and a parade. This evening we'll see a Vermeer retrospective – many tight rooms, as if viewed through a lens. You say we've lived like this for a long time, but seconds tick awkwardly on my wrist and what, after all, is 'this'? My conception of past occasions peers vaguely towards me. The future trails like a lost idea. Your hand on my injured shoulder has the fragrance of a masseur's scented oil – cedarwood and chamomile. Residual pain is the melting of coordinates.

HANDWRITING

Words on these shelves trap nineteenth-century assumptions. I enjoyed them once: an old world's vestiges made into literature; intricacies of manners and affection tied to negotiations of property. How someone removed a glove or suffered an excess of perturbation; how light illuminated a raised eyebrow in a distant room; how days accumulated a heaviness of obligation; how women mysteriously ceased being unwell. There were houses and worlds to be lost in. But now I'm looking at marginalia. Someone has written 'where were you yesterday?' next to *a little pile of glittering coin* on a page of *The Scarlet Letter*. I don't recognise the handwriting. But then there's the recollection of a hand on my hand and a scent inside breathing. I'm murmuring an answer.

SPICES

I rarely finish my jars of spices. Nor the flat packets, that lie like envelopes in a drawer. I use them all but, as they diminish, I replenish the supply. New cinnamon sticks smell like a benign form of desire, so I throw the old away. The fresh turmeric is mildly heady, reminiscent of a lover's generous idea. The cardamom pods are pungent as an absorbing dream. The dried oregano from Greece lurches with steepling sunshine. Sometimes I put down a novel nine or eleven pages from the end. Within reach of finishing, I don't wish to go on. It's something about the petering out of narrative; that artificial sense that things must conclude. Pasta is in the pan and chilli glistens.

GARLIC

Now is the bird settling on the balcony rail, ruffling feathers; a siren threading through the street; three girls playing raucous hopscotch on the pavement. You smell garlic and olive oil; you're turning a wine bottle's broken cork in your hand. The image of a clown at a children's party has come to mind, bending over you as his mask begins to slip. The bird takes flight; the garlic begins to brown, reminiscent of fried fish in an ancient Grecian village not far from Corinth. 'We defy the Romans,' the waiter said, as if it was happening now.

For JW

LIGHT

You could search a dictionary for days and never find a word for this light, the crash of feeling on the white wall, the colour of ambiguity she brings. Her horse stands with head in a bucket, flicking its tail; she's ridden over seven miles and eleven years, handing you a book of Eastern love poems – the author is a friend of hers. Together, you're climbing a long hill – but this time it's only language holding on. The light is from Europe, lounging on grass; a breeze stitches past and present – like a hand intertwining the meadow's blue and yellow flowers, releasing the scents.

SAP

Names are escaping or cling to the world's mouth. She searches for places where gorse straddles sand hills and clean creeks widen; where the tongue's mobilised by unrecognisable speech; where, with sap-sticky hands she may plant a heritage into black earth. She peers under oleanders, waits next to a tree's twisted bole, near a feinting waterfall. Her affection sniffs at recognition – old scents and obscure flavours. It knows skidding breezes; unfurling sunrise; the cracked, scoured land; a crescendo of reef and sea. And clover, sorrel, luminous forests of kelp.

For PM

MINERAL SALTS

The lounge room's stillness is memory – a white dog pants, lolling tongue brushing the floor. Blinds protect the sash window, and light and circumstance angles – as the dog waits for practised games. Its fur smells of sand's mineral salts and brown shadows under saltbush. It hears small cries and clumping feet on a boardwalk. A girl lies with a tartan blanket and shouts rise near water; a boy swims into an agitated sea. A woman twists her hands; a man in a cream suit raps at the door. Water flurries from a tap and a gate clangs. Stroking the dog, we look away from what it knows.

WOOD SMOKE

A smell of wood smoke; slow-cooking aromas and their interrogations. We had fished despite a running tide; the balcony was an escarpment falling into loss. You spoke of alienation, how increasingly you felt at one with the stony hills. The view showed scrub like knotted fur on an animal's arched back; you lifted whole fish onto plates, spoke of swimming beyond the reef. 'My daughter told me....' We could barely see each other; your words were smoke in our vision.

BITTER LEMON

Sunlight escapes from flustered curtains, striking a floor. The lemony aroma of cake absorbs the afternoon. A girl reads *Lady Chatterley's Lover*, thinking of *primroses and the first violets, that smelled sweet and cold and the anemones bobbing their naked white shoulders*. Later she straddles a boy from down the road, hitting and kneading his arms. She inhales the scent of pine, curls fingers into dirt. She finds black, wormy shade and pulls herself into a hiding place, where sounds of adults are stray as chirruping birds. A cat walks with upright tail; a possum gathers a tree under its feet. She talks to ants and crushes some with her fingers – hints of bitter lemon and ripe, coppery cheese.

FUMES

A face looks through dimensions and vanishes inside a song. The photograph album closes; time resumes a contemporary shape – even as the past circles like a bird climbing wind. Music's carried from a city so distant we forget the subway that produced it and how many coins we threw into an open violin case. The musician's bow continued to stroke the strings; car fumes were a blue swirl. The tune wavered and gusted into distance. We find a residuum, gathering our past skins on the swooping melody, holding youthful postures, unwrapping a piece of jamón ibérico: piquant smells and flavours; blood-remembered passages.

LIPSTICK

Rot, soil, a rubbish heap; bitter morning wind; words that taste of last night's wine; hens making noise. Years like this. Onions are chopped and fried; parsley's fragrant green stains a board; sliced chillis drop seeds; a cheese wheel softens near the stove. Long windows blur...

Mrs Jones warms cheese on the single heater. Outside the classroom, in two remaining bottles, discarded milk begins to clot. A visiting teacher smells of unwashed shirts. Behind the demountables eleven-year-old girls are testing lipstick. The bell summons last lessons. 'I will if you will.' Cherry on sipping lips.

WALLS

As new walls straighten, we begin to lose others that glimmered so long with lamplight. We settle into furniture's solidities – green upholstery; a startling carpet in red and blue – but they hardly belong to who we've been. You peel an orange, conjuring an oval where someone exhorts a team of children. You pick up a pen and the urge to rewrite a decades-old letter itches in your fingers. A parade of stilt-walkers passes in the street, which smells of twenty-five centuries – of drains that pass through an ancient Roman piazza. 'Let's go out,' you say. We pass election posters and eat at a café. You recollect the city – a palazzo we visited; a woman we helped; locals who bought us yeasty beer; rented rooms failing to hold our speeches.

LANGUAGE

When you enter the light, you might be entering water. When you enter the water it falls about you like light. When the young man you were steps into your skin, the breeze is from 1978. But it no longer smells of the same earth. A woman dressed you in a hundred shouts and you didn't know how to maintain conversation. So many failed attempts shadow your thought, like long, thorny boughs by a river. The light wasn't easy to find; when it arrived it nearly drowned you. And water dazzled your sense of yourself, skipping as it was with facets. Or was it the language you tried that repeatedly failed to speak for you?

VINYL

We emerged, each an insect from its chrysalis, hazy in morning light. To be outside our parents' world, stepping onto a train, gathering warm vinyl stickily onto legs. It wasn't any great satisfaction but we wouldn't forget it – breathing diesel-smelling air, leaning with elbows on cool window glass, chewing gum. We watched small shops and factories pass; we gathered the fractured world into our ken. And we mapped the city as if we'd never seen it. Staggers of skyscrapers; a welter of faces and postures; the yellow perfume of girls across the aisle. We grasped light like squares of chocolate; our thrown shadows refracted and multiplied. The train veered left just as we looked right.

CUPS

An unwieldy series of spaces that no architect planned – domes, courtyards, spires and annexes; people facing away; rain that doesn't wet the street. No-one's able to lift a top hat from an apartment floor; a line of transparent ants crosses a smoking barbecue. The smell is powerful but it's the wrong one. The whole place teeters but nothing much falls – just a few cups from a sideboard – and they were broken before.

FOLD

We explore this envelope of knowing, and it broadens into extravagances of sight – a room with exquisite cornices; a vista of plains seething with blue wildebeest. Ancient cities stand as if reconstituted – an emperor holding court; a library of lost classics. We wonder if unwritten ways become us, nostalgia inscribing different imaginaries as present hours press. Hunters round up animals; Alexander's torch lights Persepolis. Its gold-inked scripts curl, his conquests closing knowledge like a fold. We turn away from the blaze and smell of burning.

For CA

FURROW

In the black-throated cry of a single raven; in light that falls through the drip of dawn; in smells of hay in the hand-stretched field. So much speaking dives in a furrow and won't be heard; so much knowledge knows not enough; so much trying labours poorly. Here's a resumption of earth and rock and the high-toned currawong like a bend in air.

AROMA

I was emboldened by the quest for an exquisite aroma. Not bread or brioche or freshly made coffee (those smells were merely a daily harvest). Not the clothes of my lover with her sweet-sour perfumes, or the incomparable smell of her intimate flesh – I'd grown used to our pliable love. Not cut grass, or surf, or the fat pigs of Spain (that inimitable smell of jamón on the bone). Not the lovely freshness of new-printed books, or the washed-cotton fragrance of towels in the sun, or the chlorine from pools enlivening skin. Not the darkest of cocktails, or honeyed sweets, or damp, acid loam underneath tall pines. It was the air from a lake high in the alps, almost a nothing; a dissolution of blue – thirty years to locate this desire. A hint of bellflower and carniolan lily, a sense of gentian out of sight, a wind that holds snow, a taste of regret, and a keening for loss that fails to settle.

PERFUMERY

In Florence we found a perfumery, down three stairs and past a small café. Hundreds of fragrances carrying the exotic – some like sweet drinks (smelling of what we spilled); or unripe guava; or icy peppermint. Others were piratical spice – sails clapping in swathes of air. A few were alleys among green-tinted stone; one showed white-dressed nuns ambling towards prayer. A yellow bottle suggested a geranium bed. Another possessed the intimacy of a wardrobe. Two announced dissent, like unfurled flags. A rectangular bottle released an unwieldy speech. Three kept the eucalypt playgrounds of primary school – pungent, irreverent secrets.

SOUND
Paul Munden

'the plash of the fountains in their mossy niches
had lost its chill and doubled its music'
—*Henry James*

'I'm an analog man in a digital world'
—*Joe Walsh*

54	Almost inaudibly
55	On the corner of the square
56	Franz Liszt
57	Paul's letter to the Corinthians
58	You can see the music
59	The village hall film club
60	A body of water
61	Molten bronze
62	Only by its absence
63	During her lessons
64	For everyone not inside your head
65	He began to wonder
66	Listening back
67	You feel your way
68	Her letter
69	The improvised breaks
70	We slip from the back of the boat
71	As you enter the shop
72	Poor Nimbus
73	He looks for somewhere
74	Opening the drawer

ALMOST INAUDIBLY

she taps her fingers on the matchbook a friend once bought her in Sunset Boulevard, and bends the match in the open book before pulling it loose, and striking it – just for the whisper, too gently for it to catch – then striking again with greater purpose, listening for the crackle of air as she lights the candle in the tilted jar as a prelude to her words...

ON THE CORNER OF THE SQUARE

an elderly Venetian had set up stall with his glass harp: wine glasses filled to different depths, so that when he ran his moist fingers across the various mouths, they would each produce their singular note – and together, a clear-voiced harmony that carried to where we sat with our bellinis, eating blue cheese crostini... his quick looping hands conjured Vivaldi (his breaths the fleeting dips of his fingers into water) even as the waiter was carrying a Quattro Stagione to our table, the music held in the evening air... and when, years later, although the man on the corner had gone, we sat in the same square and the same waiter brought us a menu that hadn't changed, and raised our glasses – mine half empty, yours half full, G♭, F♯ – his clear movements still reflected there, ringing in our ears

FRANZ LISZT

hurries in a post-chaise towards his next triumph: Caroline de Saint-Criq; Bettina von Arnim; Charlotte von Hagn; Marie Duplessis; Marie Pleyel; Lola Montez; Olga Janina; Pauline Viardot-Garcia; Emilie Merian-Genast; Caroline Unger-Sabatier; Eveline Hańska; Agnes Street Klindworth; Sofie Menter; Baroness Olga von Meyendorff; George Sand; Princesses Carolyne von Sayn-Wittgenstein and Cristina Trivulzio di Belgiojoso; and the countless countesses, Maria von Mouchanoff, Adèle Laprunarède, Rosalie Sauerma, Marie Cathérine Sophie d'Agoult   just listen to those fingers play!

PAUL'S LETTER TO THE CORINTHIANS

is the first of the antiphons, speaking to itself across the years for the three who have worn the same Irish lace, pitching *charity* (though today it's love) above mere *sounding brass or a tinkling cymbal*... later, after the short walk home, I listen to my own speech come back to me in a foreign tongue, and two Best Men make their stereo jokes before Sicilian and English song do friendly battle in the huge, fire-lit tent at the top of the field... this is the future, you tell me when the wedding breakfast is done – these multicultural bonds and their vociferous delight – and the band gives way to an iPod pumping its eclectic playlist late into the night... it will be one or maybe two in the morning that a policeman comes to quibble but then, seeing the noise is purest joy, responds with an affirmative retreat

YOU CAN SEE THE MUSIC

in how they move, as if underwater, in the silent drift of stained glass light, a single tribe with ears like an insect's compound eyes, through which a choice of wireless soundwaves is delivered to their brains, then their muscles, without respite, so that when any one of them makes it to the bar, she shouts, convinced you can't hear her *VODKA AND TONIC!*

for AZ

THE VILLAGE HALL FILM CLUB

has subtitles that give captions for every scripted noise [sigh] [chuckle] [roar of wind] [an aeroplane overhead]... looking around I see the audience are mostly tolerant, even appreciative; our ears have grown larger by the years, to little effect, but here we can rely on the literary approximation onscreen – the text sometimes outsizing the actors' gestures or the significance of the sound

A BODY OF WATER

breaks on the shore, pulled / by the moon, knowing just when / it must swell to a crest and / dash itself again / in a rhythmic dissolution / that's equally a re-gathering, / driven by the wind / or lulled... / / listen to each wave as it approaches, / hauling enough mass at least / to revise its ponderous surges / for your distraction, as you sit alone / with your thoughts, on the sand, / holding your knees to your chest

MOLTEN BRONZE

pours into the channel between cope and core, until it fills the whole ghostly, silent space where the false bell once held sway, the design laboriously pictured with wax... it's cooling here in the sandpit for a week, before the mantle and the outer mould are raised on a pulley and the vast bell hoisted from the inner mould to be tuned on a lathe, the partial frequencies – hum, prime, tierce, quint, nominal – all brought into harmonious accord, with no going back once the metal has been ground and a single strike-note achieved, be it a summons, a toll, or part of a peal; but don't fool yourself that the pitch will be the same for you, for me, here, there, from one day to the next...

ONLY BY ITS ABSENCE

do you notice the slow pulled tick of the grandfather clock, and its hourly chime, like the daily freight train that rattled past your bedroom window, waking you with its silence that morning it didn't come, but you don't yet know how the absence will grow, when the clock, no longer just wound down, is sold, and the house sold too, a whole life gone, and something clamours to be there, with the colossal force of a waterfall implausibly frozen in the air

DURING HER LESSONS

a small boy sits under the grand piano, an outlaw hiding in the shade of a dark tree, happily doing nothing but watch the girl's bare legs with their white ankle socks and buckled blue shoes, dangling, his mother's in stockings that cling to her plump white thighs... he listens to the tentative, repetitive mistakes, and then – when his mother takes charge – the full power of the music in the canopy overhead: *the boom of the tingling strings*; the sheriff's posse on the gallop

The Boom of the Tingling Strings is a work by Jon Lord, its title taken from a phrase in the poem 'Piano' by DH Lawrence.

FOR EVERYONE NOT INSIDE YOUR HEAD

it's a seething irrelevance: the rush of white water over the horseshoe falls; the surf that pounds you to the ocean floor in a sandblasted panic; cicadas in full frenzy, beating your eardrums with their buckling timbals; the Fizzy boys revving in the street, adolescence smoothing to a manageable hum, like nostalgia; the comfort of an old valve wireless before the tinniest transistor radio replaces it with yet more excruciating off-beam hiss; white noise from the synth circa 1981; a thicket of snakes; the first feint crackle of fire, like water tipped onto gravel, or crumpled tin foil, while you wait for the inevitable whoomph; the persistent wasp that won't let you alone, zooming in your face all afternoon while the other guests doze or are peacefully lost in their books; the Formula 1 drone, lap after tedious lap; the aeroplane's engine that won't let you sleep, on a journey that won't end

The Yamaha FS1-E, affectionately known as the 'Fizzy' was a popular 50cc motorcycle of the 1970s.

HE BEGAN TO WONDER

if his poems were each set in a certain key: this one, for instance, in C♯ minor, as he lay with nothing but his darkest, most restless thoughts, a moonbeam drifting in through the roof-light on what was always her side of the bed, needling his sleep with a relentless, mournful, broken chord... the haunting was still present when he woke, his fingers slowly rippling on the pillow beside his face

LISTENING BACK

over his recordings, he could just make out a blackbird joining in, and was pleased – not just with the unexpected act of community, but the genuine harmony produced, and as he listened to his various attempts at the new song in different keys, he was astonished to hear how the blackbird re-pitched its counter melody to the guitar, and he abandoned the song, staring out of the window in search of his casual accomplice, who'd moved on

for NB

YOU FEEL YOUR WAY

across the bedroom in the dark, your memory gauging the distance between one piece of furniture and the next, to the door, the stairs, and you think of Mr Lecky, survivor of that unnamed catastrophe, prowling the department store in which he is trapped... it's the script they would return to, Peckinpah and Silke, whenever there was time to kill, falling into their old routine ('he'd get the meats, I'd get the peanut butter and bread, we'd fight over the ice cream'), facing their own demons, digging deeper at the story, digging so deep there was no way out, making *Castaway* their reality... and every sound comes to haunt you: a squirrel scratching at the moss on the roof, the creak of a shrinking pipe, the bark of a dog long dead, and the clock, the clock that tells you this isn't a dream, that you won't wake up

Sam Peckinpah's abandoned adaptation of *Castaway*, the novella by James Gould Cozzens, is scheduled for production in 2019.

HER LETTER

is unopened in his green jacket pocket as Leo is hurried on his way by your fugue – across a field, a fateful summer, England, the past, or is it the future – through the heat, a new century, a thirteenth birthday (unlucky for some), and as he pauses by the tree we fear the worst, for all the beauty of your nouveau baroque; the music is the go-between for the boy you once were and the man who reads that counterpointed, breathless, 'darling darling darling' on the page

(i.m. Michel Legrand, 2019)

THE IMPROVISED BREAKS

were already out of hand, but now the bow begins to thrash against the strings, its flayed filaments drifting in a haze of rosinous dust, a savagery fuelled by Polish spirit, stretching the music to the point that it must surely snap... it hangs by a shred, the spot-lit figure writhing on the floor, the violin somehow still gripped between shoulder and chin, the bow finding space to do more damage, and as we hold our breath in the dark, there's a moment of calm, which could almost be mistaken for defeat, the end, but it's the silence in which everything turns – *a twitch upon the thread* – and we watch the crumpled figure uncurl, the music cradled after all, brought back from the brink, tiny gasps of melody making themselves known once more, feeling their way before hurtling towards relief

WE SLIP FROM THE BACK OF THE BOAT

into the ocean and tread water with our fins; it's a dress rehearsal, in wet suits and snorkelling masks, the crew assessing our competence in the open sea for when the humpbacks approach, and we are doing ok, but really we are poor, poor creatures, ill-equipped for our research, our survival, even our play, because today – for the first time in nine months of the year – the visibility in the water won't do and the crew are shaking their heads: we're not safe; and all the while some forty whales are gathering around us, their delicate grunts and soundings so precise they might even sense our dismay

for FED

AS YOU ENTER THE SHOP

all sound is humbled into abeyance, the walls lined with box-shelved balls of coloured wool, from floor to ceiling, a soft rainbow waiting for your needles, your plan... the voices that push their way through the quiet are from the past, themselves the pull of wool through wool: your aunt in her lilac cardigan; your grandma searching for buttons in a drawer; but one comes to mind as slightly more shrill, a mother-in-law making a point – about darning, socks, *darning wool – where do you get yours, these days?* – at which you look around, dumb

POOR NIMBUS

would never belong, not while the black Bakelite phone was there in the corner of the hallway, beside the Chinese vase of umbrellas, though for hours he looked for all the world full of calm, if a little subdued; inside he quivered with a terror he couldn't explain, or describe, waiting for that phone to come alive, the first trill rippling through his body and causing a frenzy in which he jumped and tore every curtain from its hooks… you only knew of it through your parents' stories – how the mayhem was a cycle, the curtains replaced, torn down, replaced, torn, replaced, the little corgi in a whirlwind of shredded nerves – until such time as a new home could be found, one where he could see each conversation emerge, hear it for what it was

HE LOOKS FOR SOMEWHERE

to place the Lafont Guarneri del Gesù on which Adolf Brodsky premiered the Tchaikovsky, and chooses the open grand at which Janusz Olejnicak is taking his seat, and you think *surely not*... the varnish on this fiddle is no mere gloss; its layers embody the history of its play, the ever-richening tone of a performative life, heritage made audible... and now he's looking for somewhere to put his bottle of beer, and you think *please please God no*...

OPENING THE DRAWER

he finds a jumble of old cassettes, some labelled, some not; some in the wrong hard plastic cases (some of them broken, or cracked) – Blondie masquerading as Verdi, *The Enigma Variations* as *Aladdin Sane* – and a blank one proving to be *By Jeeves!*; an indistinct recording in an Eastern European accent (from a lecture? the radio?) about melting ice-caps is a mystery; then there's music he wrote himself, and his own voice reading poetry on the BBC... it's a catalogue of surprises, the level of startlement destined to fall – until he stumbles on the pencilled date, *31st October, 1981*... and as he slips the forgotten tape into the deck and presses play, he hears not only a famous toccata, but a pivotal six minutes of his life, the breathy detail of that autumnal afternoon, a ritual concluded, everyone making their way from the church to where the music stops

THE SIXTH SENSE
Jen Webb

> 'Comme si les mots, les phrases
> Étaient en nous organes
> D'un sixième sens.'
> —*Eugène Guillevic*

> 'this secret buried in reeds at the beginning of sound I
> won't let go of man, under
> his soakaway ears and his eye ledges working
> into the drift of his thinking, wanting his heart'
> —*Alice Oswald*

78	Read between the lines
79	The medium is the message
80	Child's play
81	Proprioception
82	Blindsight
83	In Canaan
84	Poltergeist
85	Attendant
86	Diagnosis
87	What I meant to say
88	Making the wood pile
89	Trees
90	The third degree
91	Old truths
92	Political aides
93	Dream worlds
94	Water and cloud
95	Feral
96	Hamelin
97	Alice's counsel
98	After midnight

READ BETWEEN THE LINES

You catch a glimpse. An impression of light at the corner of your eye. Someone was there, and then gone in a breath. On the office wall a sign reads 'We prosecute trespassers' but no one prosecutes the green man. CCTV shows only static; and when Security asks what you saw, you merely shrug. If you too could pass unobserved; if light would take you in its hands. But it bounces off the cracked surface of the wall, scatters against the buildings, and the streets shift improbably under our feet. Subtle but certain reminders that all we have is fleeting. We will mail each other postcards, tiny gestures toward permanence. We will tell each other that nothing changes, even as buildings slide under the sea, as the postcards crumple and blur. No one promised a blissful transformation but if you close your eyes, slowly, and slowly cease your breath, then what marvels.

THE MEDIUM IS THE MESSAGE

People you may know include: Joe Livingston, Eva Caccatoria, Phyllida Thomas. If you tap the correct answer you may well have won a new phone. You worry over your old phone, tapping at its screen, complaining that it's changed, that it used to be so good to use. Meantime your UberEats order is closing in on you, a cartoon bicycle jagging its way through the CBD toward you and this tiny studio in an old building where you dare not touch banisters or door handle with naked hand. Great location, said your friends, but isn't it small? And then, over drinks: what's happened to whatshisname? People you may know include: Peter Underhill, Gloriana Bose. People you may know include Tony Freebase, Martin Bikes. You phone me, late at night. You say it's strange, isn't it. It's all so strange.

CHILD'S PLAY

He is making a tower of clouds, because ninety per cent of everything is visible to no one. Up it goes, academic paintings from the nineteenth century stacked on memory cards from his grandmother's funeral and on model aeroplanes he has never built. Working only with his fingers and a shimmer at the corners of memory, he takes one and one and makes his tower, and beside it piles pomegranates four deep, glowing, and beside them the bone handled knife with its ground-fine blade that is older than any of us. It grandfathers the picnic basket, startles the berries. He tests its edge, then puts it down, carefully, on the kitchen bench.

for Angus

PROPRIOCEPTION

Seeing without sight, because he can't see. The power has shut down again and the moon too is blank, and clouds obscure the cobweb light of stars, and he falls over the furniture, treads on a cat. On the other side of day she is standing on unanchored steps, looking across to where the hills are just beginning to turn blue, imagining how she will leave, pack a little bag, walk until she gets there. A *there* she will know when she meets it. The sun dips, the steps sway under her feet. He reaches out, she reaches out, but the spirit level in the spine has cracked. He is wrist deep in darkness, and she is falling.

BLINDSIGHT

Mist seeps into record books, wrecks the upholstery, rusts the trees. It turns sister against sister, mother against son. No one can confirm how the budget stands, no one parses the president's words. So she closes her eyes, urges every other sense to attend to the world that taps its knuckles on her head. Listen to the sound of blue; trace the shape of coffee; taste the death metal that spills over the fence from her neighbour's son's bedroom. The factory has closed. Shop fronts are cracked, clouds press down on her and the walls have turned to ruin – spikes on the tongue, splinters in the eyes. A lover's hand on her thighs. Now her fingernails are bleeding from the struggle. She turns wearily from the fight. We will never win, she says. We'll never win.

IN CANAAN

There were snakes beneath the bed, two or dozens or tens, and the dogs snarled and yowled and the farm workers fired salt at snakes and beat the dogs with sticks. We stood on our beds, clinging to each other, watching. Because it's true, you know this now, the ground really can open up and swallow you whole. Swallow you, and whole houses, and territories. At night, beneath my bed, I hear Mr Death coming to find me; and you, my cousin, my dear, standing on the bed, beckoning me.

for GC

POLTERGEIST

A house full of people sleeping, and you, prowling. The things you'd do if you were half as bad as they say. You flick through the mail they have left on the counter, remove photos of children from their frames, reformat the computer. Working silently, such small crimes, more annoyance than ruin. Someone is shouting out in his sleep, calling your name. Have you wriggled through the filters and into his dreams? The door opens, and closes.

ATTENDANT

Between house and hill I lost the sense of you. At night I woke, and glanced at whoever was sleeping beside me. There is always someone there; there is always something going on. The tap on the shoulder, the stranger between the sheets. I walk through the underpass that leads to the station and backlit kiosk windows speak to me, softly and slurred. Someone is sleeping in my bed. I want them gone, and me alone. Someone is walking beside me, then ahead: a shadow. When it fills out beneath the street lights, it takes on your shape. And at the end of all this, when we have made our peace and said our long goodbyes, know that it will always be me, standing at the front door, listening.

DIAGNOSIS

It comes on you. Losing solid memories, you rehearse your morning lines. Doctors call it hypertension, specialists say there's something awry in the wiring. Whatever it is, you don't know and can't know.

To be honest, he said, I'm not that keen. She kissed him, hard, tongue in throat. *How about now?* she asked as he stumbled back. Pause.

It rolls in. Pull over to the side of the road, say *hang on just a minute sweetie* if you're busy with the kids, or you're busy with your lover, or you're walking the dog. It's awkward as hell, sure, but better to take the careful way.

When red comes, it swarms all over you. No one in their right mind would hold you accountable for what happens next. It's myth. The only true story. And you? You are dog. Still hoping to have your day.

WHAT I MEANT TO SAY

When I lose sight of you, still I can smell you – smoking weed out on the balcony, burning leaves on the garden path. Indoors we have a kind of speaking: me wriggling out of my clothes, showing myself only as skin; you reaching out, awkward, missing me entirely. We never do find the rhythm. Our friends have parsed the sentences of touch; we alone still fumble through the phrasing. 'The pen of my uncle', 'the garden of my aunt'. What new grammars must we learn? Sing your way through it: whistle like a bird, click like a frog, sound the depths of sound and make no meanings. Comme ci, comme ça. Shout it out, darling: you only live once.

MAKING THE WOOD PILE

There was just one place where the voices fell silent: at the saw he'd set up beyond the chook run, beside the wood pile, where for twenty minutes or fifteen hours he could cut dead trees into wood, headphones muting the racket of wind through the wire fences, of hens singing or sheep calling out or the nazgul cry of cockatoos. Haul. Cut. Stack. And repeat. Sun on his back. Muscles bruised. Wood pile growing. If he could maintain the pattern, his voices would be stunned into silence, and his wife and children stay safe another day.

for AB

TREES

She is out again, wandering the unlit streets, pausing to place the palm of her hand against a tree. The suburb is leafy; she is spoilt for choice, every few metres, each side of the street. She takes care not to think what might be in the shadows they cast – spiders, or dogshit, or man. If you hold still, she tells her doctor, you can feel the pulse of plants, tree-blood running beneath the surface of skin. On moonless nights she prefers not to dwell on it. Drawing the darkness around her, a cape. She sits on the pavement, feet in the gutter, eyes on the sky.

THE THIRD DEGREE

Why there is something, not nothing. That's statement not question, so I won't reply. Now it's my turn: *Why are there windows?* You heave yourself out of your chair, drag the curtains closed, slap palms on the coffee table. You say *Because.* The wine glasses jump. *Now stop fucking doublethinking me.* And you change the game: Where were you on the night of? Who were you thinking of when you called out in your sleep? Who was it phoned and your face lit up? You fucking candle. I will blow you out.

OLD TRUTHS

The moon is stalking us, but I am mostly water, you are chalk. You have been casting your net across the globe. Lean in close instead; everything that is in me will lean in to you. The moo. That solitary eye, that cool gaze. I am small, and broken, and flawed. If I reach out, your face will press against my hand. Cold stone. My companion beast, my strange enemy. If only we could find what we had before, when you were lovely, and far away, before we watched all the old saws coming true.

POLITICAL AIDES

We work opposite sides of the street and passing, I touch your hips. Paused at the street lights you place your hand across the small of my back. Markers of connection, lovers who dare not speak their name. In the deep night I open the curtains a crack and undress, slowly, the light behind me, knowing you are waiting outside, as you do whenever you can break free. Born in the wrong year, raised in the wrong land, still we leave trails of breadcrumbs for each other, hesitant gestures toward a better future.

DREAM WORLDS

The languages rattle through you. Images hunch and brood, and you dream, in several tongues: (wanneer u 'n klein droom gedroom, of 'n nagmerrie... uphupha? ... dream a little dream ...). Listen to the bell. Ask what happens next. It's too soon to tell: you are still in dreamland, in long fields that change to shifting sands. You are describing circles on tussock ground, you are looking for the way out, for a new town where houses have been sketched by children on a chalkboard, where your strangeness passes unremarked, where nothing matters not even the rain.

WATER AND CLOUD

I am racing to you, slowly, in a car I don't know. Outside Auckland the traffic thins and air comes more easily, the sky folds its wings back, and as I hit Tainui country that old taniwha starts its witching: cars thicken on the road ahead, then vanish as I approach. The traffic swells and ghosts, swells and ghosts. Wait for me. I'll make it to you, soon. You will be standing outside, or dozing in a chair. You will framing photos, or watching the water in the lake below the home. The lake matters still, and I matter, even if you can't remember my name.

FERAL

We were living out in dry country, where neighbours said our land housed panthers, or pumas, or lion. The experts said nonsense but hunters laid out rancid baits, hunkered themselves down in hides with cameras and blankets and beer. The big cats came, they said, and paused like ghosts before the hides. The big cats came, and posed. The photos failed, their spoor and scat blew away. The hunters left, disconsolate. Months later and miles from their camp I watched as something walked calmly past: black points, yellow eyes, haunches low and narrow. Ever since, when light moves in a certain way, I see the world move too, and I smell my own skin: feline, and rank.

HAMELIN

You go out, trying to catch the shadow that is always cast ahead. Hunting by night, being stalked during the day. You cycle down the narrow roads between forests of teenaged trees, narrow-waisted, swaying together, and when you try to catch them out, they freeze in place. *What's the time Mr Wolf?* In the garden children are dancing fairy rings. Shadows shift, strangers step in and out between the shuttering shadows, you could be the Pied Piper and they your followers, leaving one dimension, finding five.

ALICE'S COUNSEL

You are tumbling down the rabbit hole, grasping at air. She is putting you to the test, asking *what is the word for that feeling you get when your eyes blur and you see only shadows on your skin?* Dread, you say, and she nods. Then: *Children coughing in the night?* Asthma, you say, I expect. And then: *White wine that tastes of limestone?* Pass. Which means: fail. You could make up a name, but what would be the point. She is checking her phone, glancing across the room. She asks, *What is the word for when you are falling, and the ground is nowhere near, and all you can do is speak out the names of things you know?* You don't answer; all you know is that naming gives us nothing, not even the ground under our feet.

AFTER MIDNIGHT

The moon has gone. The neighbours are asleep and the cat stands, and stretches, then begins to wash. Look outside: something is moving across your plane of sight – night bird, or runner, or the floating worlds inside your eyes. If you could reach the keys. If you could find your phone. Peel back your skin; step naked onto the street. All that is left is terrain: the cartography of the body, its deserts and its bays, your future picked out in sand.

TASTE
Jordan Williams

Impossibility, like Wine
Exhilarates the Man
Who tastes it; Possibility
Is flavorless—Combine

A Chance's faintest Tincture
And in the former Dram
Enchantment makes ingredient
As certainly as Doom—

—*Emily Dickinson*

102	Bitter
103	Sweet
104	Salty
105	Sour
106	Aroma
107	Umami
108	Good
109	Bad
110	Astringent

BITTER

At first, all I know is fear of falling, of snakes, of losing my way. On the single track, I settle into a rhythm, leap and zig over rocks and scat. Air blown down over the mountain and across the river valley rises up, cleaner and colder now, shocks my lungs. By the fifteen-minute mark, pungent decay mixed with sweet new grass from a rare rain forces me to pay attention to where I am above what I'm risking. Chalky tracks torture up through dry scrub and take me with them. My legs become logs and I slow to a walk and spit out bitter dust as I watch other runners glide ahead. Still, I'm here, drinking it all in as the wallabies watch.

SWEET

Her lipsticked lips would taste of plum if he could get her alone and kiss her. He would lick her tattoos and the nape of her neck and find some new appetite. He was sure of it. She was solicitous smiles and honey phrases and her laugh was golden. And now her voice is a sharp caw that cuts him dead. Her breath has a sour note that he can't quite place but it's from a time and place he wants to forget. Her lips are still plum. Her laugh is still warm. But she is all surface and gloss.

SALTY

I bore the mounting pressures of academic life by consuming ever larger doses of salt in an attempt to restore balance. I started by adding small amounts to the usual foods. But the metallic taste of imminent failure still coated my tongue, my gums, the membranes of my mouth. After my annual review (it didn't go well – I'm not enough) I found myself salting strawberries and other sweet things to keep myself grounded. Small dishes of flavoured flakes, smoked, truffled, matcha, were dotted around the house so I could gather up the crystals on a moistened finger and touch their sizzle to my tongue. Anything for a bodily sensation. After all this time I am partially preserved in a state of anxiety about what might happen if... I dare not look back to the good old days.

SOUR

The sourdough, the mother, bubbles and separates and I add more teff and water every other day. I run the same route on Wednesdays and Fridays, Winter and Summer. Small rituals are the weak rhythm measuring the pulsating madwoman. Like the mother, I inevitably separate into layers, a sludge and a piss coloured liquid. Like the mother, I need to be attended to by shaking but also by addition of the basics that are not always on hand. Tending myself is a lonely business and the mother often turns bad.

AROMA

The wheels behind my eyes become visible to me by some random trick of the light bouncing off your mirror shades. I can smell the oily engine grime and hear the clunking of my gears as abstractions are formed and extruded slowly. It's all very rough and pre-modern and I can't discern what's fuelling it – instead of steam there's a cold fog that's a recipe for rust. You appear to be looking straight into my eyes as if you can hear it too. But that impression is a function of the angle of your head and the slant of your worldview. In reality you're asleep back there, nothing going on. I whir on, amusing myself no end, while people do what people do.

UMAMI

My bitterness, your kindness. Your pessimism, my belief in light. A shared reticence transmogrifies into a tsunami of nowness, each elevating the other in this strange friendship. A rainy day beside the algal lake, the only two determined enough to commit. Then you drove me further and further beyond the safe boundaries of habit and sometimes now I fly as we commit crimes against logical limits. We are umami – each stands alone but combined we are more.

GOOD

So much of the world makes no sense to me and I would truly like to understand. Two visitors who drink neither tea nor coffee yet live in Melbourne. A man who's held a grudge against vine leaves for forty years. And what makes a woman with Puritan long hair horrified enough to comment on mine, her mouth puckered like a prune? Or a woman who pays no attention to her own dress take the time to perform shock at mine? Posturing in the name of good taste is not in good taste.

BAD

There are mornings when I still crave bacon, but vegan meats perplex me with their nostalgia for abandoned practice. Still, I've sought an analog bacon I can believe in but no go. A pig I know reminded me that they are also known to eat their young, like gluttonous humans who eat their emotions without ever tasting a thing. Overconsumption is always in bad taste except in maximalist fashion and, of course, books.

ASTRINGENT

Your first meeting – you saw him salivating and you knew you were for it. His appetite was triggered and he still belittles you at every turn. You burn, you shrink, you collapse in on yourself. It is not enough to abrade you, he dabs your flesh with vinegar and begins again. You look trapped in this cycle of torture and occasional soothing sounds but don't you want to escape? Run home and wrap yourself in olive oil and cotton gauze. After a while you will be able to distinguish between good and evil although you'll never again know the highs of open wounds or the lows of being ignored.

CITE

STATEMENTS

Cassandra Atherton

The human sense of **touch** is 'the first sense to develop in the womb and the last sense one loses with age' and yet it is often the most overlooked of the senses (Krishna 2012: 335). There is a special intimacy associated with touch because our skin is required to make physical contact in order to register touch – and, unlike the other senses, we have the ability to sense touch all over our bodies. This is one of the reasons why the somatic pleasure of touch has serious consequences when it is unwanted or forced; when it is a negative touch.

This chapbook addresses the sense of touch as primal and takes as its inspiration the report from Swedish researchers Line S Löken et al in 2009 who exposed neurons to 'soft slow touch' and recorded 'for every spike in voltage there was a small but predictable increase in pleasure' (2017: n.p.). The prose poems in this chapbook aim to recreate these 'spikes' as lovers' touches.

Furthermore, as fingerprints have become metonyms for identity, this chapbook also investigates touch through a postfeminist frame, discussing the way in which – despite the sexual revolution – 'slut' is:

> a warning more than a word – a reminder to women that we must adhere to the narrow standards of femininity and sexuality set out for us, or be punished accordingly. And in that way, the real meaning of 'slut' is terrifyingly clear. (Valenti 2014: n.p.)

This chapbook is a celebration of lovers. It makes intertextual use of both Roland Barthes' *A Lover's Discourse: Fragments* (1977) and Maggie Nelson's *Bluets* (2009) to explore powerful responses to sex through the charged utterances of love and heartbreak. At times, the chapbook is both earnest and irreverent, playing with taboo while exploring the sensitivity of fingertips.

Stephen M Phelps asks, 'Can we learn how a fleeting touch drives a frenzied heart, or why the delay between contact and withdrawal can span a decade? An answer worthy of our effort should begin at the skin's surface, yet somehow end in poetry' (2017: n.p.). This chapbook honours that notion, presenting a suite of prose poems that are a kind of exploratory beginning as well as an end.

Works cited

Barthes, R 2010 [1977] *A Lover's discourse: fragments* (trans R Howard and W Koestenbaum), New York, NY: Hill and Wang

Krishna, A 2012 'An integrative review of sensory marketing: Engaging the senses to affect perception, judgment and behaviour', *Journal of Consumer Psychology*, 22 (3): 332-51

Löken, LS, Wessberg, J, Morrison, I, McGlone, F, & Olausson, H 2009 'Coding of pleasant touch by unmyelinated afferents in humans', *Nature Neuroscience*, 12 (5), 547-548

Nelson, M 2009 *Bluets*, Seattle, WA: Wave Books

Phelps, SM 2017 'Touch', *Aeon*, 4 April 2017, at https://aeon.co/essays/it-takes-neuroscience-and-poetry-to-map-the-tributaries-of-touch

Valenti, J 2014 'What makes a slut? The only rule, it seems, is being female', *The Guardian*, 23 June, at https://www.theguardian.com/commentisfree/2014/jun/23/slut-female-word-women-being-female

Paul Hetherington

In considering the importance of the sense of **smell** in human prehistory, Italo Calvino writes, 'We understood whatever there was to understand through our noses rather than through our eyes … the world is in the nose' (2012: 71). Although this claim may be something of an exaggeration, even in the contemporary post-industrial world we rely on our sense of smell a great deal – and what we smell, and what we know through smell, affects and inflects our experiences in myriad ways. Smell is arguably the sense that contributes most importantly to early memory development because of the 'uniquely privileged neuroanatomical relationship between olfactory processing and the structures that govern emotion, memory and associative learning' (Herz 2012: 109). Many of the smells of childhood stay with us throughout our lives, whether this is the smell of soil, the fragrance of blossoms, the odours carried by breezes or the perfumes of soap and washing powder.

During childhood we also encounter numerous other smells, such as those associated with sweat, grass, clothes, furnishings, animals, damp, fire, sunshine, bodies of water and rain. Through these encounters we make a kind of mental map of our local odours and fragrances and our domestic environments – and of human connections, too. A favourite aunt may be associated with the smell of a leather armchair; or a neighbour's house may be tainted by the smell of diesel from a generator. We relish food partly because of how it smells – and what we usually call taste is partly made up of what we smell. We associate desire and love with the individual smell of particular bodies. Smell is also a major factor in recognising what is healthy or unhealthy. For instance, we understand rot and death partly through the powerful smells of decomposition.

Some scents are encoded within memory in such a way that, decades after meeting someone, we may be reminded of them if we encounter the perfume they wore. The smell of sausages cooking at a particular barbecue may tantalise us years after the event. Even whole cities smell of themselves – which is to say, of their environs, history, buildings and human habitation. For instance, mid-summer in Rome has a redolence that belongs to no other city, suggesting millennia of human habitation. If a visitor dislikes that redolence, then parts of Rome in mid-summer may be unpleasant. But if the city's occasionally pungent aroma suggests warm and pleasingly intimate associations, one may live with a fond idea of Rome and its characteristic smells for a lifetime.

Holly Dugan writes that 'smell is culturally and biologically central to human life, yet it often seems enigmatic'

(2011: 2) and that quality, too, helps makes the sense of smell entrancing. One does not always quite know what a particular smell may be or what it suggests or is reminiscent of. Indeed, as Fredrik U Jönsson and Mats J Olssen note, human beings often have trouble naming an odour, and they suggest that this may be because the 'simultaneous processing of olfactory and language information leads to interference' (2012: 118). Certainly, the sense of smell interacts with language in sometimes challenging or problematic ways. We cannot always confidently name a smell except through linking it with something tangible and nameable – and, even so, the experiences associated with certain smells may remain elusive. Recognising this, the prose poetry in this volume explores different ways to connect language, smell and meaning poetically (and metaphorically). In doing so, these works examine smell's potent role in our constructions of meaning and memory, and its continuing significance to a great deal of what we do and understand even as we age.

Works cited

Dugan, H 2011 *The ephemeral history of perfume: Scent and sense in early modern England*, Baltimore, MD: Johns Hopkins University Press

Calvino, I 2012 *Under the Jaguar sun* (trans W Weaver), New York, NY: Houghton Mifflin Harcourt

Herz, RS 2012 'Odor Memory and the special role of associative learning', in GM Zucco, RS Herz and B Schaal (eds), *Olfactory cognition: From perception and memory to environmental odours and neuroscience*, Amsterdam/Philadelphia: Jon Benjamins, 95–114

Jönsson, FU and Olssen, MJ 2012 'Knowing what we smell', in GM Zucco, RS Herz and B Schaal (eds), *Olfactory cognition: From perception and memory to environmental odours and neuroscience*, Amsterdam/Philadelphia: Jon Benjamins, 115–135

Paul Munden

The theme of these new prose poems connects, inevitably, with my previous set on *Rhyme* (Munden 2018), and here the relationship between 'topic' and 'fabric' is even more primal. **Sound** is of course fundamental to poetry, even when silently there on the page or being read without utterance. We see its sound even before we convey it on the air, a form of synaesthesia at work, and the nature of its sonic artistry is what convinces us of its content; indeed, the two are sometimes indivisible.

There is a complex connection between the sounds in a poem and the sounds in the world to which it relates. Writing about the 'moss'd cottage trees' in Keats's 'Ode to Autumn', FR Leavis suggests that we 'hear' the bite through an apple (1962: 16). Despite Terry Eagleton's quibbles with this (2007: 59), I would maintain that it is hard *not* to hear that crisp bite once the idea has been planted. And if exposure to such 'incarnational fallacy', as Eagleton calls it, has 'disadvantaged' me (ibid.: 68), it is a position from which I have consistently enthused in poetry, both as reader and writer. Perhaps I am fan of 'displaced onomatopoeia', as I would prefer to call it.

In a prose poem, sound sits within – and emerges from – its space in a different way to a lineated poem. Contemplating that, and building on previous attempts at the form, I have made specific use of the poem's 'mould' to represent the spatial (or metaphorical) confines of the 'event'.

As previously, I have included references to film, the directors this time being Peckinpah (again) and Joseph Losey, whose adaptation of LP Hartley's *The Go-Between* (with Harold Pinter, 1971) makes manifest the connection between memory and music. There is a sense in which music can make memory audible. I have written elsewhere (Munden 2017) about the prose poem's elastic treatment of time, and in these poems I focus on the crucial role of sound in that process, the ability of sound to transport us in time, as it does so poignantly for Proust (1922–31), a garden gate bell sounding across the years, and featuring as the framing device for Pinter's *Proust Screenplay* (1978).

If music – sound in its most elevated sense – dominates the poems' attention, I have focused on somewhat unusual occurrences (wine glass Vivaldi, a silent disco) and music of the natural world, indeed of ordinary life – what Seamus Heaney, borrowing from James Stephens (1920), describes in his poem 'Song' as 'the music of what happens' (1979: 56). It is through sound above all that '[t]he poem constitutes the very things it is about' (Eagleton 2007: 69). Keats, in his 'Ode on a Grecian Urn', writes that 'Heard melodies are sweet, but those unheard / Are sweeter' (1970: 209), and among the many intriguing aspects of that phrase is the fact that, for a poet, sound is simply not expendable, even in referring to its absence.

Works Cited

Eagleton, T 2007 *How to Read a Poem*, Oxford: Blackwell Publishing Ltd

Heaney, S 1979 *Field Work*, London: Faber & Faber

Keats, J 1970 [1820] *Poetical Works*, Oxford: Oxford University Press

Leavis, FR 1962 *The Common Pursuit*, Harmondsworth: Penguin

Munden, P 2017 'Playing with time: Prose poetry and the elastic moment', *TEXT*, Special Issue 46, at http://www.textjournal.com.au/speciss/issue46/Munden.pdf

Munden, P 2018 *Rhyme*, Canberra: Recent Work Press

Pinter, H 1978 *The Proust Screenplay*, London: Eyre Methuen

Proust, M 1922–31 *À la Recherche du Temps Perdu*, Paris: Grasset and Gallimard

Stephens, J 1920 *Irish Fairy Tales*, London: Macmillan

Jen Webb

There is no **sixth sense**, declares Aristotle, though for centuries it was understood as the sense that engaged stimuli beyond the known, that stood in for what cannot be articulated: the extra-sensory, the poetic (Heaney 1995), and the numinous (Pearson 2015). Science, of course, drives out magic, and has re-defined the sixth sense as physiological function. It is identified as the immune system, for example – a sensory organ that attends to what is below the range of the other senses (Blalock 2005); it represents presence, or how the brain attends to the barrage of sensory signals in a place (Slater 2002); more probably, it is the other name for the vestibular system, which organises movement in and through the world (Goldberg et al 20012), and provides vision that does not rely on the retina – or 'blindsight' (Berthoz 2000). But beyond science, a hint of its old magic remains: the sixth sense, even in its most experimental and empirical sense, is the sensory mode that attends to what cannot be seen with the naked eye; what is still under investigation; which hums the ineffable. These 21 poems attempt to wrestle with the various meanings for the sixth sense – to express the experience of what appears only when the curtain of the world shifts. The other sense of the sixth sense comes to us from the sixteenth century, and the *Lady and the Unicorn* tapestries, five of which bear the title of one of the conventional senses – sight, sound, smell, taste, touch. The sixth tapestry bears the phrase *À mon seul désir / My only desire*. This, the inexplicable sensibility of yearning and desire, is a further and final meaning for the sixth sense that is explored in these poems.

Works cited

Heaney, S 1995 *The Redress of Poetry: Oxford Lectures*, London: Faber & Faber

Pearson, R 2015 'Strategic gaps: Poetry and the sixth sense from Chateaubriand to Mallarmé', *Dix-Neuf* 19.2: 113–29

Blalock, JE 2005 'The immune system as the sixth sense', *Journal of internal Medicine* 257: 126–138

Slater, M 2002 'Presence and the sixth sense', *PRESENCE* 11.4: 435–39

Goldberg, JM et al 2012 *The Vestibular System: A Sixth Sense*, Oxford, Oxford University Press

Berthoz, A 2000 *The Brain's Sense of Movement*, (trans G Weiss), Cambridge, MA: Harvard University Press

Jordan Williams

The tongue holds receptors for each of the five main **taste**s: sweet, sour, bitter, salty and, the most recently added to this taxonomy of tastes, umami. The tongue, our mouths. Such an intimate and culturally loaded space. Everyday functional, erotic in some cultures, erogenous. This is the centre of tasting. And taste became the metaphor for aesthetic judgement, perhaps because to taste food we must distinguish between tastes, perhaps because it was considered that a balance in the tastes of food was required for good health as was balance thought to be important for beauty. My poems – Sweet, Sour, Bitter, Salty, Umami, Good, Bad and Astringent – seek to recount the association between those tastes and everyday life and relationships.

ABOUT THE POETS

Cassandra Atherton is a prose poet and Associate Professor in Writing and Literature. She was a Harvard Visiting Scholar in English and a Visiting Fellow at Sophia University, Tokyo. She has published 17 critical and creative books and edited special editions of leading journals. Cassandra is the successful recipient of many national and international grants including VicArts and Australia Council Grants. Her most recent books of prose poetry are *Pika-don* (2018) and *Pre-Raphaelite* (2018). She is co-writing a scholarly book, *Prose Poetry: An Introduction* with Paul Hetherington (Princeton University Press) and co-editing *The Anthology of Australian Prose Poetry* (Melbourne University Press).

Paul Hetherington has published and/or edited 27 books, including 13 full-length poetry collections and nine chapbooks. Among these are *Moonlight on Oleander: Prose Poems* (UWA Publishing, 2018) and *Palace of Memory* (Recent Work Press, 2019). He won the 2014 Western Australian Premier's Book Awards (poetry) and undertook an Australia Council for the Arts Literature Board Residency at the BR Whiting Studio in Rome in 2015–16. He was shortlisted for the Kenneth Slessor Prize in the 2017 New South Wales Premier's Awards and commended in the Surprise Encounters: Headstuff Poetry Competition 2018 (Ireland). He is Professor of Writing in the Faculty of Arts and Design at the University of Canberra, head of the International Poetry Studies Institute (IPSI), and one of the founding editors of the international online journal *Axon: Creative Explorations*. He founded the International Prose Poetry Group in 2014.

Paul Munden is a poet, editor and screenwriter living in North Yorkshire. He has published five poetry collections, most recently *Chromatic* (UWA Publishing, 2017). He was director of Poetry on the Move, 2015–2017, and director of the UK's National Association of Writers in Education, 1994–2018. He has worked as conference poet for the British Council, reader for Stanley Kubrick, and script writer/editor for GSP Studios. He is a Royal Literary Fund Fellow at the University of Leeds, and an Adjunct Associate Professor at the University of Canberra. He is co-editor with Shane Strange of *Giant Steps*, an anthology marking the 50th anniversary of the Apollo 11 moon landing (Recent Work Press, 2019).

Jen Webb is Dean, Graduate Research, and Distinguished Professor of Creative Practice at the University of Canberra. The ACT editor of Australian Book Review's States of Poetry anthology, co-editor of the bilingual anthology *Open Windows: Contemporary Australian Poetry*, the literary journal *Meniscus*, and the scholarly journal *Axon: Creative Explorations*, she is also author of several poetry collections and artist books. Her most recent poetry collection is *Moving Targets* (Recent Work Press, 2018).

Jordan Williams is an educator and researcher who works in multiple media, mainly textiles, video and poetry. Her work, practice and creative research, reflects an abiding interest in vulnerability and isolation and the anxiety that both leads to and is magnified by them. Her higher education research focus concerns how creative arts practice can alleviate the suffering brought about by illness and injury. She has designed programs in creative writing for and mentored injured and ill military personnel and people from communities affected by drought.

IPSI: INTERNATIONAL POETRY STUDIES INSTITUTE

The International Poetry Studies Institute (IPSI) is part of the Centre for Creative and Cultural Research, Faculty of Arts and Design, University of Canberra. IPSI conducts research related to poetry, and publishes and promulgates the outcomes of this research internationally. The institute also publishes poetry and interviews with poets, as well as related material, from around the world. Publication of such material takes place in IPSI's online journal *Axon: Creative Explorations* (www.axonjournal.com.au) and through other publishing vehicles, such as Axon Elements. IPSI's goals include working – collaboratively, where possible – for the appreciation and understanding of poetry, poetic language and the cultural and social significance of poetry. The institute also organises symposia, seminars, readings and other poetry related activities and events.

CCCR: CENTRE FOR CREATIVE AND CULTURAL RESEARCH

The Centre for Creative and Cultural Research (CCCR) is IPSI's umbrella organisation and brings together staff, adjuncts, research students and visiting fellows who work on key challenges within the cultural sector and creative field. A central feature of its research concerns the effects of digitisation and globalisation on cultural producers, whether individuals, communities or organisations.